Shifting Perspectives

Contents

Features

For much of her life Helen Keller was unable to see, hear or speak. Read **Help at Hand** on page 12 and learn more about her remarkable life.

You've probably heard of surfing ocean waves, but have you heard of surfing airwaves? Read **Free-Falling Photographer** on page 18 for more.

Do you fail to see things that are right before your eyes? Do you sometimes see things that aren't there? Try **Eye Tricks** on page 22.

Some people think that grey hair and wrinkles are signs of beauty and wisdom. Some people want to look young forever. Read **Beauty Is in the Eye of the Beholder** and join the debate on page 28!

What does it mean when someone has "eagle eyes"?

Visit www.infosteps.co.uk
for more about ANIMAL EYES.

Windows on the World

The human eye may only be the size of a table tennis ball, but for most people the eye is a complex machine that feeds information to the brain at lightning speed. Using the five main senses of sight, hearing, smell, taste and touch, the brain constantly processes data about the world around us. It is the sense of sight, however, that feeds the brain with the greatest volume of information.

Unlike most animals humans have eyes that face forward—set in the front of the head rather than one on each side. Our eyes are constantly on the move, gazing skyward to follow a bird as it arcs across the sky, zooming in to track the movement of an ant across the ground and darting from side to side as we cross a road. The eye can spy the flicker of a candle up to one kilometre away and can distinguish colours and a vast range of shades.

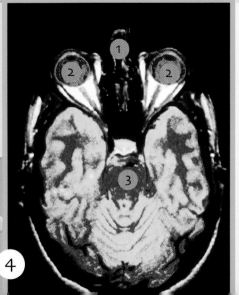

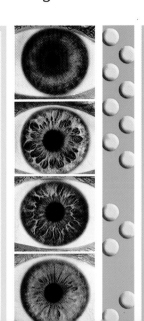

The picture at the left shows a scan of a head from above.

1 Nose

2 Eyeballs

3 Brain

4

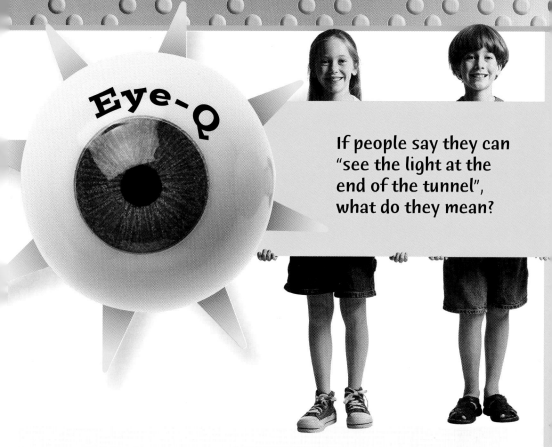

Eye-Q

If people say they can "see the light at the end of the tunnel", what do they mean?

The eye does not actually see objects. Instead it sees the light that objects reflect. Light is a form of **electromagnetic** energy that travels in varying wavelengths, or phases. We are able to see seven colours in the wavelengths of visible light. Many animals do not see the same colours in light rays as humans do.

Eyeballs Exposed

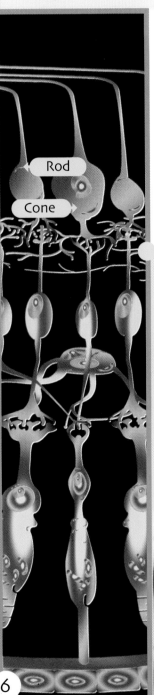

Rod

Cone

Human eyes are a little like miniature fluid-filled video cameras. The soft squishy eyeballs are well protected, nestled in bony eye sockets and able to hide behind eyelids fringed with lashes that help keep dust and debris from clouding vision. Six muscles move each eyeball every time we shift our gaze.

The retina is covered with light-sensing cells called rods and cones. Rods detect movement and cones detect the colours red, green and blue. Variation in light causes different combinations of these cones to produce all the colours we see.

Light bounces off every object our eyes encounter. The light enters through the clear dome-shaped cornea at the front of the eyeball. It then passes through an adjustable hole called the pupil, that lies at the centre of a ring of muscle called the iris. A lens focuses the rays of light so that they cast a detailed upside-down image on the retina, which lines the back of the eyeball. Here the image is transformed into millions of electrical signals that hurtle along the **optic** nerve to the brain, where it is interpreted and read right-side up.

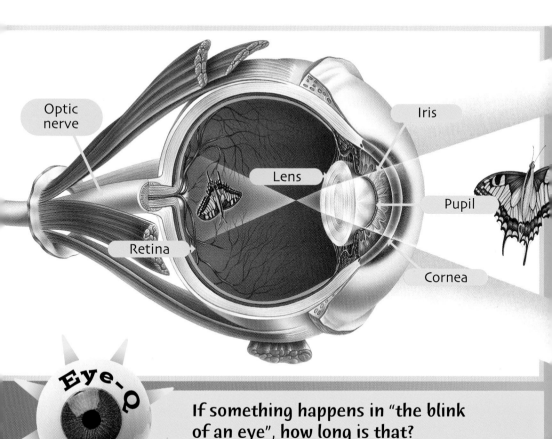

Optic nerve

Iris

Lens

Pupil

Retina

Cornea

Eye-Q

If something happens in "the blink of an eye", how long is that?

When Sight Isn't Right

Problems with vision often occur when an eyeball is out of shape. If an eyeball is too long the lens is unable to focus on faraway objects, causing a person to be near-sighted. If it is too short it causes a person to be far-sighted. If the cornea has lost its domed shape and fallen flat it causes astigmatism, making objects both near and far appear blurry. These common eye defects affect a large number of people.

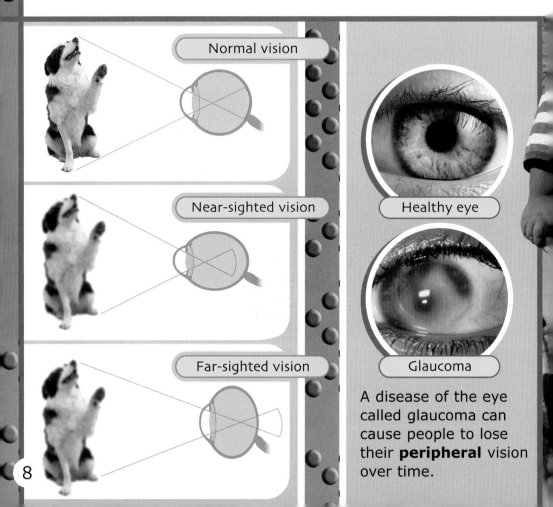

Normal vision

Near-sighted vision

Far-sighted vision

Healthy eye

Glaucoma

A disease of the eye called glaucoma can cause people to lose their **peripheral** vision over time.

Some people suffer from a far greater degree of vision loss, however. Partially blind people have very limited vision, while totally blind people are unable to tell light from dark. Disease and accidents are the main causes of blindness.

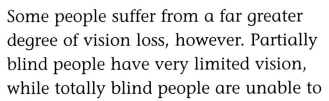

If people are "seeing red", what emotion are they experiencing?

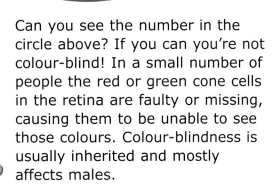

Can you see the number in the circle above? If you can you're not colour-blind! In a small number of people the red or green cone cells in the retina are faulty or missing, causing them to be unable to see those colours. Colour-blindness is usually inherited and mostly affects males.

9

High-Tech Eye Tech

There are many ways to correct flawed eyesight so that people are able to have a more accurate picture of the world around them. Prescription glasses were invented during the 1200s to help people with near- or far-sighted vision. Contact lenses were developed over the following centuries and laser surgery during modern times.

People suffering from blindness need more help than glasses or surgery can provide, however. Guide dogs are trained to help blind people get out and about and a system of reading and writing called Braille keeps blind people in touch with the outside world.

Braille was invented by a Frenchman named Louis Braille in 1829. It uses a combination of raised dots to form letters and words that can be read by touch. It grew out of a code used in the military that allowed soldiers to read battle plans at night without light.

Time Line of Bright Eye-deas

1200s The Europeans and the Chinese invent glasses.

1440 The printing press is invented and reading becomes a popular pastime. By the mid 1500s wearing glasses is high fashion!

1508 Artist and inventor Leonardo da Vinci has the idea of contact lenses, but people do not yet have the technology to make them.

1784 Benjamin Franklin invents bifocals because he is tired of changing his glasses for close-up reading with his glasses for distant viewing.

1851 Scientist Hermann von Helmholtz invents an instrument called an ophthalmoscope that allows doctors to see inside the eye.

1887 The first contact lenses are produced. These are made of glass and are too painful to wear for more than one hour.

1938 The first user-friendly contact lenses made of hard plastic are produced.

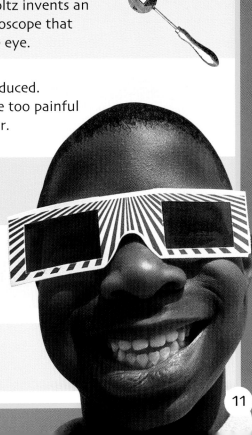

1970s Soft contact lenses made of flexible plastic are produced.

Late 1900s Laser surgery and eye implants improve many people's vision.

Help at Hand

Helen Keller (1880–1968) was a person who knew, perhaps better than anyone else, how it is to live in complete darkness, without light nor shadow nor even sound. Born in the US state of Alabama, Helen was a normal healthy baby. She spent her days as any curious toddler does, exploring the world around her, speaking her first words, looking, listening, tasting and touching. At nineteen months of age, however, Helen suffered a terrible fever that left her totally blind and deaf—alive but alone in a dark silent world that no one could enter.

When Helen was almost seven a brave and determined young woman named Annie Sullivan came to work with her. Having suffered from poor vision herself Annie was expert at reading Braille and at signing. She used her fingers to spell words into the palm of Helen's hand. By using the sense of touch Annie began to connect Helen with the outside world and Helen began to form pictures in her mind.

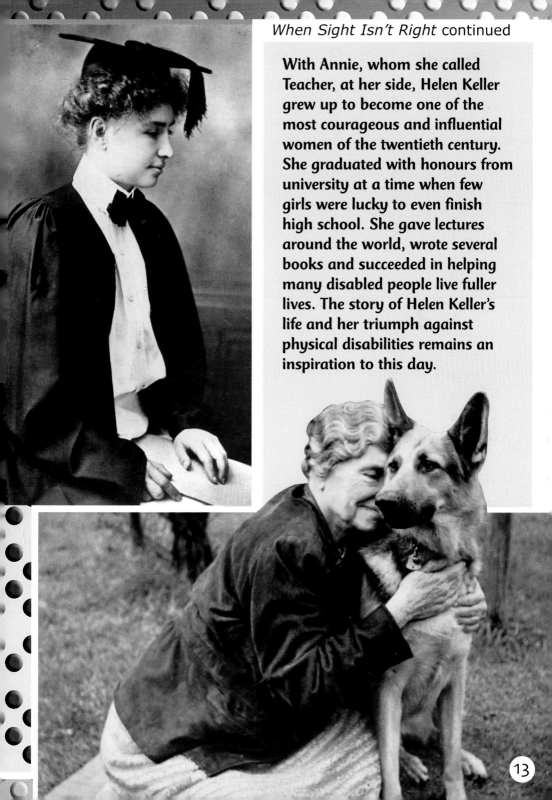

With Annie, whom she called Teacher, at her side, Helen Keller grew up to become one of the most courageous and influential women of the twentieth century. She graduated with honours from university at a time when few girls were lucky to even finish high school. She gave lectures around the world, wrote several books and succeeded in helping many disabled people live fuller lives. The story of Helen Keller's life and her triumph against physical disabilities remains an inspiration to this day.

Eye Spy

Zoom In

It can be true to say "what you see is what you get" about some things, but most things have hidden and intricate details that lie beneath their surfaces or beyond the power of the naked eye. Over the centuries great thinkers have predicted the presence of objects they were unable to identify due to the limited technology of their time. These things were as yet unnamed and often the very suggestion of their presence went dangerously against the accepted beliefs of the time.

People have now invented many tools to help us see objects in a new and more detailed way, allowing us to have a greater understanding of our world.

Match Them Up!

TRY THIS!

A

B

C

D

E

1

2

3

4

5

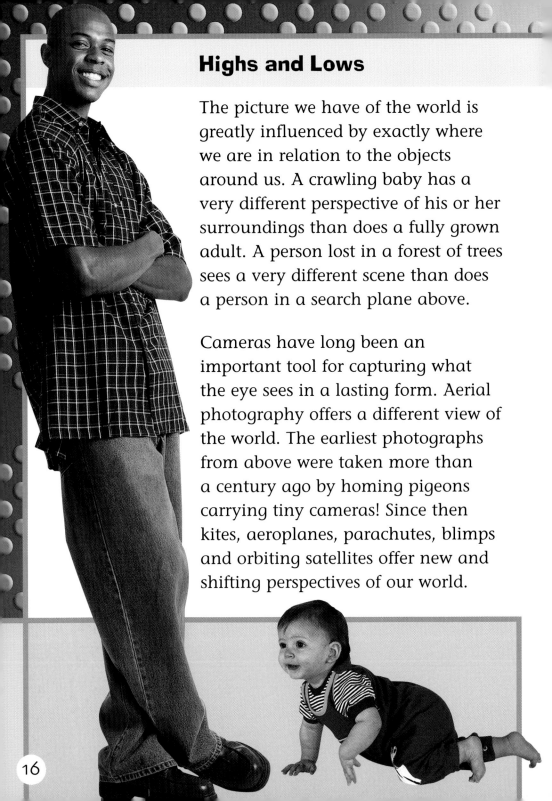

Highs and Lows

The picture we have of the world is greatly influenced by exactly where we are in relation to the objects around us. A crawling baby has a very different perspective of his or her surroundings than does a fully grown adult. A person lost in a forest of trees sees a very different scene than does a person in a search plane above.

Cameras have long been an important tool for capturing what the eye sees in a lasting form. Aerial photography offers a different view of the world. The earliest photographs from above were taken more than a century ago by homing pigeons carrying tiny cameras! Since then kites, aeroplanes, parachutes, blimps and orbiting satellites offer new and shifting perspectives of our world.

Eye-Q

If you "see eye to eye" with someone, what is happening?

SITESEEING · PLANTS & ANIMALS ·

What does it mean when someone has "eagle eyes"?

Visit **www.infosteps.co.uk**
for more about **ANIMAL EYES.**

Free-Falling Photographer

Wendy Smith is thought by many to be the world's number one female camera-flyer. Wendy began skysurfing when she was 17 years old. Since then she has completed more than 12,000 jumps, leaping out of aeroplanes to fall at speeds of up to 250 kilometres per hour!

Over the years Wendy has worked as a stunt skydiver for commercials. She began to take her own camera on jumps and experimented with free-fall photography. Now Wendy travels around the world photographing world-record skydiving competitions and filming for movies.

Through a combination of supreme skills, technical know-how and sheer creative flair, Wendy succeeds in presenting a whole new perspective of the world.

On Assignment

Q Wendy, what made you want to skydive?

A *I took my first flying lesson when I was 16 and have always loved aeroplanes, so it seemed natural for me to jump out of one!*

Q What has been your most memorable moment?

A *There have been many moments in the 12,000 skydives I've completed, but I will never forget my very first tandem skysurfing jump stunt.*

Q How has your view of the world changed by seeing it from so high above?

A *I can see things changing quickly on the ground over a large area from this high altitude. Each jump is fresh and different and never fails to leave me feeling totally in awe of nature's incredible colours and forces.*

Optical Illusions

Sometimes our eyes play tricks on us. They can miss things that are in plain view. They can see things that are not there. To a person in the heat of the desert rippling waves of light can look like a pool of water or an oasis. This optical **illusion** is known as a mirage. It is a result of the brain trying to make sense of the information it receives.

From mirrors that distort an image to 3-D glasses and virtual reality games, people have invented many ways to trick our eyes and fool our brains.

Magicians are experts at fooling our brains. They use tricks of the trade to distract our attention and pull off a startling surprise right before our eyes!

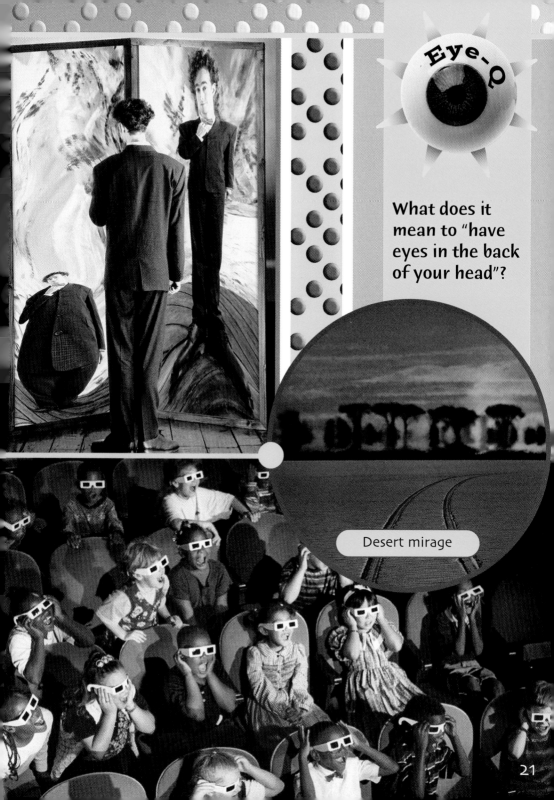

Eye-Q

What does it mean to "have eyes in the back of your head"?

Desert mirage

Eye Tricks

Do you see an old lady or a young woman?

Do you see a woman's face or a man playing a saxophone?

Do you see a vase or two faces?

There are no light receptors in the area of the eye where the optic nerve leads to the brain. This means that every eye has a blind spot. See if you can find your blind spots by trying the eye trick below. First cover your left eye and focus on the white dot. Then hold the book at arm's length and slowly bring it closer to you until you can no longer see the black cross. Now cover your right eye and do the same thing while staring at the black cross until the image at the left disappears.

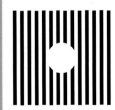

+

Imagine that you had
to make this impossible
object. How are your
eyes fooling you?

Are you seeing dots
before your eyes?
Are the dots black or
white? Can you tell?

Are the red lines
curved or are they
straight and parallel?
How could you check
your answer?

Which colour
arrows do
you see first?

Are the parallel
lines the same
length? Check
your answer.

An Eye on Art

Artists are experts at tricking the eye through the clever use of mathematics and lighting to create an impression of depth and space. A talented artist succeeds in making a flat two-dimensional painting come alive in such a way that it seems the viewer could reach out and touch the objects on the canvas. M.C. Escher was an artist famous for using geometric designs and optical illusions to create pictures full of perplexing perspectives and impossible scenes. He was a master of the visual **paradox**.

Look closely at this picture by M.C. Escher. What is strange about it?

A view from above puts a different perspective on a crop art version of Vincent van Gogh's famous painting of sunflowers. Driving a red tractor, artist Stan Herd etches *Sunflower Still Life* out of a clover field in Kansas. His work will grow in texture and colour as the soybean and sunflower seeds sprout and mature.

Eye-Q

What does it mean when someone wants "an eye for an eye"?

25

The Mind's Eye

The way we see and interpret the world has a great deal to do with our attitudes and values. While two people living in the same place at the same time may share very similar experiences they will never see events in exactly the same way. Because of their individual life experiences and their personal hopes and expectations people will always have different perspectives, or points of view.

Same time.

Same place.

Same game.

What is the winner's point of view?

What is the loser's point of view?

There's More than Meets the Eye

Every person is an individual. When you put a person in a general category based on just one characteristic such as gender, age, appearance or occupation, you are creating a **stereotype**. What stereotypes can you identify in these pictures?

27

A Changing Outlook

Even widely accepted beliefs can change over time as new information causes perspectives to shift. In the 1500s, for example, many people began smoking because they believed tobacco was good for their health. Today we know that smoking can cause death so our attitude towards it has changed. We also know now that hygiene is very important for good health. Long ago some people believed that keeping clean was a health hazard!

WHAT'S YOUR OPINION?

Beauty Is in the Eye of the Beholder

In many parts of the world grey hair and wrinkles are signs of wisdom. Where I come from it seems that people try hard to look forever young and "beautiful". Many dye their hair. Some even have facelifts or plastic surgery.

My grandma looks old, but I think she is very beautiful. She says she has a story behind every grey hair and every wrinkle! I never get tired of her stories and maybe I've even given her a grey hair or two myself! What are your views on age and beauty?

28

People who live during the same time, but in different parts of the world or with different cultural backgrounds will often have diverse points of view too. Our attitudes and values are usually influenced by the people we are closest to—our family members, our friends, our schools, our community and the leaders of our nation. In many cultures the media and the advertising industry also have a strong influence on people's outlooks and attitudes.

Eye-Q Revealed

- To see the light at the end of the tunnel means to be near the end of a lot of hard work.

- When something happens in the blink of an eye it happens very, very fast. It takes about one-third of a second to blink your eye!

- To see red is to be extremely angry.

- To see eye to eye with someone is to agree with people or share their point of view.

- To have eyes in the back of your head is to be very alert and aware of what is going on all around you.

- When people want an eye for an eye they want the punishment to match the crime!

Glossary

electromagnetic – the force that combines electricity and magnetism. Visible light is only one part of the electromagnetic spectrum. Electromagnetic waves of energy also include heat waves, microwaves and radio waves.

illusion – something that seems to be real but is not

optic – to do with vision or the eyes

paradox – something that seems to contradict itself. A visual paradox is a picture that contradicts itself.

peripheral – to do with the outer part or edge of something. Peripheral vision is what allows you to see things out of "the corner of your eye".

stereotype – an oversimplified picture or opinion of a person, group or thing. People who stereotype others show a prejudiced attitude or a shallow way of thinking.

Index

Research Starters

1 Recheck the definition of what a stereotype is and then research magazines and newspaws to find examples of stereotypes in the media or advertising today. Write a caption to explain each example.

2 Try to understand what it is like to not see well. Choose a safe place for your experiment. Ask a friend to blindfold you and give directions so that you move around the space and back to the starting point. Describe what happened and how you felt.

3 Visit the library and look through the pictures and advertisements in really old magazines. How have attitudes changed and perspectives shifted between now and then?

4 Do you know that cats can see in the dark and bees can spot ultraviolet light? What else can you learn about animal vision?

Does this waddle or hop?